This Book Belongs To:

Discover Your Superhero Name!

January => Storm
February => Falcon
March => Invisible
April => wonder
May => sticky
June => Muffin
July => Flash
August => glorious
September => fantastic
October => magic
November => Rock
December => Force

The colour of your shirt

The object to pour left

Name Your Superhero

____

Color Your Superhero
Superhero

Superhero
Crossword Puzzle

ACROSS

3 FIGHTER
6 SAVIOUR
9 GALLANT
12 PROTECTOR
13 CULT-FIGURE
16 SUPERHUMAN
21 SUPER HERO
22 LAWMAN
23 SALVADOR
24 GODLIKE
25 HEROINE
27 PARAGON

DOWN

1 HEROIC
2 DEFENDER
4 JUSTICE
5 LIBERATOR
7 HERO
8 SUPERHEROES
10 DELIVERER
11 LIFESAVER
14 CHAMPION
15 SUPERMAN
17 LEADER
18 GUARDIAN
19 SAVIOUR
20 BRAVERY
26 RESCUER

Name Your Superhero

Let's Catch The Thief!

Help Me Find The Best Route

Response: In appendix - F

Name Your Superhero

Count The Superheros?

Name Your Superhero

Name Your Superhero

___

Can Your Fill In The

Missing Numbers?

1		3	4	5	6	7	8	9	10
	12	13	14		16	17	18	19	20
21	22			25	26	27		29	
31	32	33	34	35		37	38	39	40
41		43	44	45	46	47	48	49	50
51	52		54	55		57	58		60
61	62	63		65	66	67		69	70
71	72	73	74	75	76	77	78	79	
81	82		84	85	86	87	88	89	90
91	92	93	94		96	97	98	99	

Response: In appendix - E

CREAM

Name Your Superhero

____

Name Your Superhero

____

Superhero
Word search

```
K S T L R E D N E F E D
Z U L Q D G S O F I X S
F P A I Y U D I H Q S U
N E W V Y D G E N A B P
A R M L S H R A V R E E
M H A S T O I I A C C R
R E N E I D O V I M I H
E R R N R U E T G O O U
P O E A R R S W L S R M
U Z U W Y U I K T W E A
S G N L J U H E R O H N
V C L I F E S A V E R I
```

Words To Find

HERO, HEROINE, BRAVERY, SUPERHUMAN, GUARDIAN,
LIFESAVER, SUPERHERO, FIGHTER, JUSTICE, LAWMAN,
DEFENDER, SAVIOUR, HEROIC, SUPERMAN

Response: In appendix-A

Name Your Superhero

____

Superhero
Crossword Puzzle

ACROSS

3   XMEN
8   CAPTAINAMERICA
9   SUPERHEROES
13 FLASH
15 WONDER WOMAN
16 JUSTICELEAGUE
18 AQUAMAN
19 WOLVERINE
20 BATMAN

DOWN

1   AVENGERS
2   GREEN ARROW
4   DAREDEVIL
5   CAPTAIN AMERICA
6   GREEN LANTERN
7   BLACK PANTHER
10 SPIDERMAN
11 THOR
12 IRONMAN
14 SUPERMAN
17 HULK

Name Your Superhero

____

Can Your Fill In The

Missing Numbers?

1	2	3	4	5		7	8	9	
11	12		14	15	16		18		20
21	22	23		25	26	27	28	29	
31		33	34	35			38		40
41	42		44	45		47	48	49	
51	52	53	54		56		58	59	60
61	62	63		65	66	67			70
71		73	74		76			79	80
81		83	84	85		87	88	89	
91		93	94		96	97		99	100

Response: In appendix - E

Name Your Superhero

Can Your Fill In The

Missing Numbers?

1	2		4	5	6		8		10
11		13	14	15		17	18	19	
	22	23		25	26		28	29	30
31	32		34	35		37		39	
41		43	44		46	47	48		50
	52		54	55	56			59	
61		63	64	65		67	68	69	70
	72	73		75	76		78		
81	82		84	85		87		89	90
91	92	93	94		96	97	98	99	

Response: In appendix - E

Name Your Superhero

____

What's Your Superhero Name?

Find the first letter Of your first name:

A. Amazing
B. Magnetic
C. Fire
D. Magnificent
E. Dynamic
F. Invisible
G. Wonder
H. Super
l. Awesome
J. Turbo
K. Banana
L. Annoying
M. Chocolate
N. Vanilla
O. Strawberry
P. Stinky
Q. Secret
R. Space
S. Orange
T. Nightmare
U. Purple
V. Judgemental
W. sticky
X. Pretentious
Y. Invisible
Z. Bodacious

And the first letter Of your last name:

A. Captain
B. Wonder
C. Super
D. Phantom
E. Dark
F. Incredible
G. Professor
H. Iron
I Hawk
J. Archer
K. Steel
L. Bolt
M. Atomic
N. Torch
O. Space
P. Mega
Q. Turbo
R. Fantastic
S. Invisible
T. Night
U. Silver
V. Aqua
W. Amazing
X. Giant
Y. Rock
Z. Power

Name Your Superhero

____

Name Your Superhero

____

Let's Catch The Thief!

Help Me Find The Best Route

Response: In appendix - G

Count The Superheros?

Name Your Superhero

____

Count The Superheros?

Name Your Superhero?

Let's Catch The Thief!

Help Me Find The Best Route

Response: In appendix - H

Name Your Superhero

____

Superhero
Word search

```
C O S T U M E I R F S Z
J W T M N A M O W T A C
G W E Z A Y S A L Q W C
S W R V G S W H T L H K
R T R H N Q K L Y A F J
E E I U O I N F L Y U R
G R F G R D Y L E S A X
N C Y A T U E U T Z R K
E E I O S N Y I E R F H
V S N Y G R C D O I E Q
A U G E T E Q M M V R P
M Y S T E R I O U S L Y
```

Words To Find

MASK, COSTUME, TERRIFYING, CHALLENGE,
MYSTERIOUSLY, SECRET, STRONG, CATWOMAN,
JUSTICE, AVENGERS

Response: In appendix-D

Superhero
Crossword Puzzle

ACROSS

3. SUPER-GIRL
5. FLY
8. MYSTERIOUSLY
9. CHALLENGE
11. ICEMAN
15. FAST
16. TERRIFYING
17. COSTUME
18. WILD-CAT

DOWN

1. POWERFUL
2. RESCUE
4. RESPONSIBILITY
6. HELP
7. HUMAN-TORCH
8. MASK
9. CAPE
10. BRAVE
12. CAT-WOMAN
13. RUN
14. SMASH

Count The Superheros?

Name Your Superhero

____

Can Your Fill In The
Missing Numbers?

	2	3	4	5		7		9	10
11		13		15	16	17	18	19	20
21	22	23		25	26		28		
31	32		34	35		37		39	40
	42	43	44		46	47	48		
51	52		54	55		57		59	60
	62	63		65	66	67	68		
71	72		74		76			79	80
81		83		85	86	87	88	89	
91	92		94		96		98	99	100

Response: In appendix - E

Superhero
Crossword Puzzle

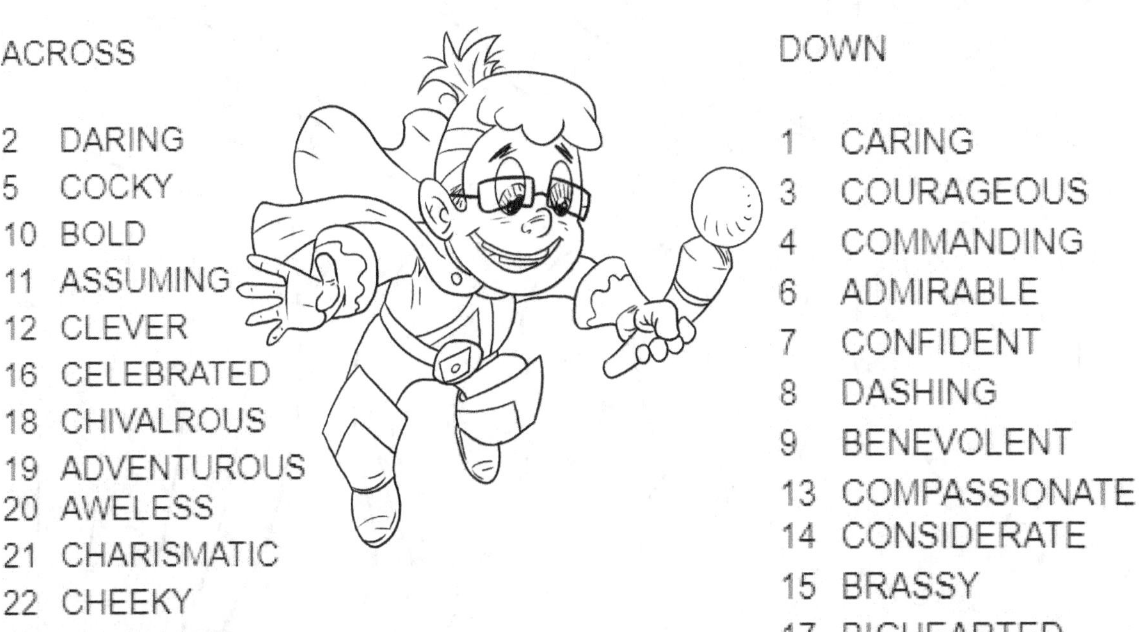

ACROSS

2 DARING
5 COCKY
10 BOLD
11 ASSUMING
12 CLEVER
16 CELEBRATED
18 CHIVALROUS
19 ADVENTUROUS
20 AWELESS
21 CHARISMATIC
22 CHEEKY
23 DAUNTLESS

DOWN

1 CARING
3 COURAGEOUS
4 COMMANDING
6 ADMIRABLE
7 CONFIDENT
8 DASHING
9 BENEVOLENT
13 COMPASSIONATE
14 CONSIDERATE
15 BRASSY
17 BIGHEARTED

Let's Catch The Thief!

Help Me Find The Best Route

Response: In appendix - I

Superhero
Word search

```
S U P E R H E R O E S J
G P U T N A L L A G I D
O V R O D A V L A S N E
D N T W R I P F R O O L
L I F H P T R O I M G I
I A J C R E T P L R A V
K L J Z U A M E B O R E
E I L C R A A Y B T A R
S V S E H D T G N S P E
I E B C E O W O A I L R
R I Z R S A V I O U R Z
L H R O T C E T O R P D
```

Words To Find

GALLANT, GODLIKE, RESCUER, SAVIOUR, DELIVERER, CHAMPION, LEADER, PROTECTOR, LIBERATOR, SALVADOR, PARAGON, SUPERHEROES, STORM, VILAIN

Response: In appendix-B

Name Your Superhero

Can Your Fill In The

Missing Numbers?

1	2		4	5		7	8		10
11	12	13		15	16		18	19	
		23	24		26	27		29	30
31	32	33		35	36		38		40
41		43	44	45		47	48	49	
	52	53		55	56			59	60
61	62		64	65	66	67	68		70
71			74			77	78	79	
		83	84	85	86	87		89	90
91	92	93	94	95		97	98		100

Response: In appendix - E

Name Your Superhero

____

Superhero
Word search

```
Y  Y  V  Q  W  I  L  D  C  A  T  K
H  I  P  Q  M  K  A  D  H  M  M  N
K  U  L  R  I  G  R  E  P  U  S  Z
P  J  M  Z  T  U  B  S  R  Y  T  D
R  O  H  A  M  Q  M  R  N  S  L  W
P  R  W  J  N  A  B  A  A  E  P  F
L  J  H  E  S  T  M  F  U  V  N  K
E  S  N  H  R  O  O  C  J  A  E  Y
H  S  Z  U  W  F  S  R  M  N  T  D
T  Z  Y  T  R  E  U  E  C  N  U  M
C  Q  A  V  R  Q  C  L  S  H  V  R
H  C  Q  O  U  I  M  C  A  P  E  U
```

Words To Find

POWERFUL, SUPERGIRL, CATWOMAN, WILDCAT
HUMANTORCH, ICEMAN, FLY, HELP, SMASH, BRAVE,
FAST, RESCUE, RUN,CAPE

Response: In appendix-C

Name Your Superhero

____

Can Your Fill In The
Missing Numbers?

	2	3	4	5		7		9	10
11		13		15	16	17	18	19	20
21	22	23		25	26		28		
31	32		34	35		37		39	40
	42	43	44		46	47	48		
51	52		54	55		57		59	60
	62	63		65	66	67	68		
71	72		74		76			79	80
81		83		85	86	87	88	89	
91	92		94		96		98	99	100

Response: In appendix - E

Answers

Appendixes

Superhero

Word search

Response Appendix-A

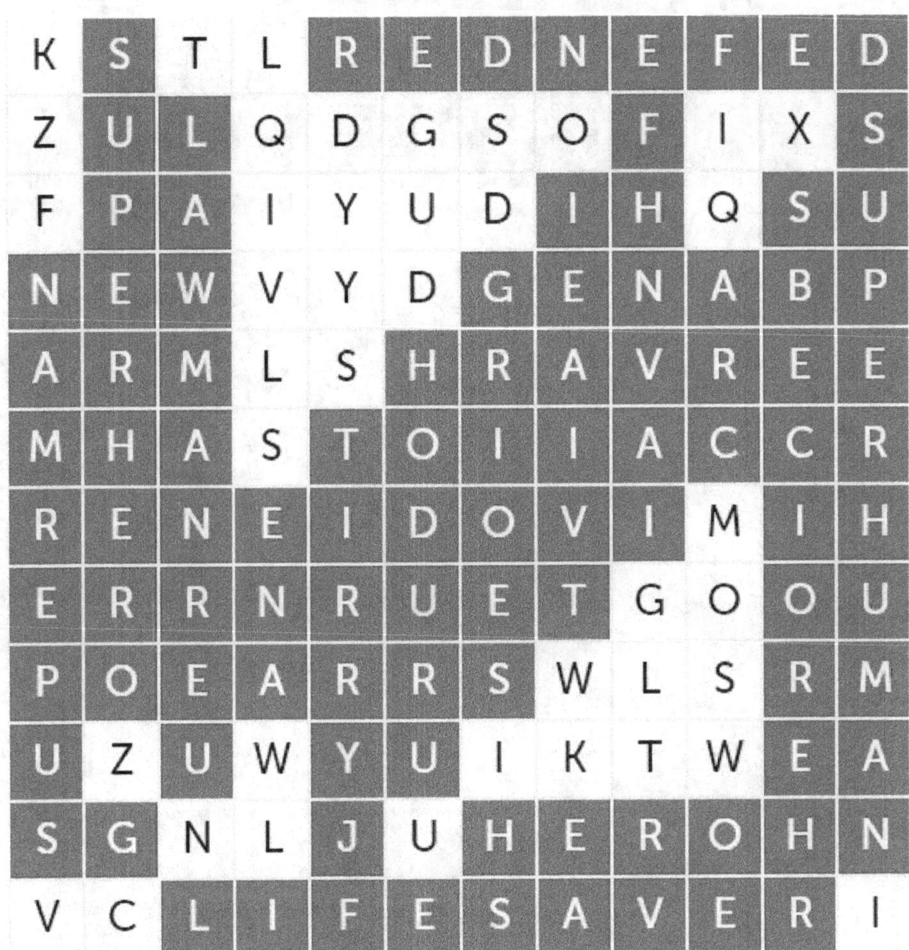

Words To Find

HERO, HEROINE, BRAVERY, SUPERHUMAN, GUARDIAN, LIFESAVER, SUPERHERO, FIGHTER, JUSTICE, LAWMAN, DEFENDER, SAVIOUR, HEROIC, SUPERMAN

Superhero
Word search

Answer: Appendix-B

S	U	P	E	R	H	E	R	O	E	S	J
G	P	U	T	N	A	L	L	A	G	I	D
O	V	R	O	D	A	V	L	A	S	N	E
D	N	T	W	R	I	P	F	R	O	O	L
L	I	F	H	P	T	R	O	I	M	G	I
I	A	J	C	R	E	T	P	L	R	A	V
K	L	J	Z	U	A	M	E	B	O	R	E
E	I	L	C	R	A	A	Y	B	T	A	R
S	V	S	E	H	D	T	G	N	S	P	E
I	E	B	C	E	O	W	O	A	I	L	R
R	I	Z	R	S	A	V	I	O	U	R	Z
L	H	R	O	T	C	E	T	O	R	P	D

Words To Find

*GALLANT, GODLIKE, RESCUER, SAVIOUR, DELIVERER, CHAMPION,
LEADER, PROTECTOR, LIBERATOR, SALVADOR, PARAGON,
SUPERHEROES, STORM, VILAIN*

Superhero
Word search

Response: Appendix-C

Words To Find

POWERFUL, SUPERGIRL, CATWOMAN, WILDCAT
HUMANTORCH, ICEMAN, FLY, HELP, SMASH, BRAVE, FAST,
RESCUE, RUN,CAPE

Superhero
Word search

Response: Appendix-D

C	O	S	T	U	M	E	I	R	F	S	Z
J	W	T	M	N	A	M	O	W	T	A	C
G	W	E	Z	A	Y	S	A	L	Q	W	C
S	W	R	V	G	S	W	H	T	L	H	K
R	T	R	H	N	Q	K	L	Y	A	F	J
E	E	I	U	O	I	N	F	L	Y	U	R
G	R	F	G	R	D	Y	L	E	S	A	X
N	C	Y	A	T	U	E	U	T	Z	R	K
E	E	I	O	S	N	Y	I	E	R	F	H
V	S	N	Y	G	R	C	D	O	I	E	Q
A	U	G	E	T	E	Q	M	M	V	R	P
M	Y	S	T	E	R	I	O	U	S	L	Y

Words To Find

*MASK, COSTUME, TERRIFYING, CHALLENGE,
MYSTERIOUSLY, SECRET, STRONG, CATWOMAN, JUSTICE,
AVENGERS*

Answers

Appendix E

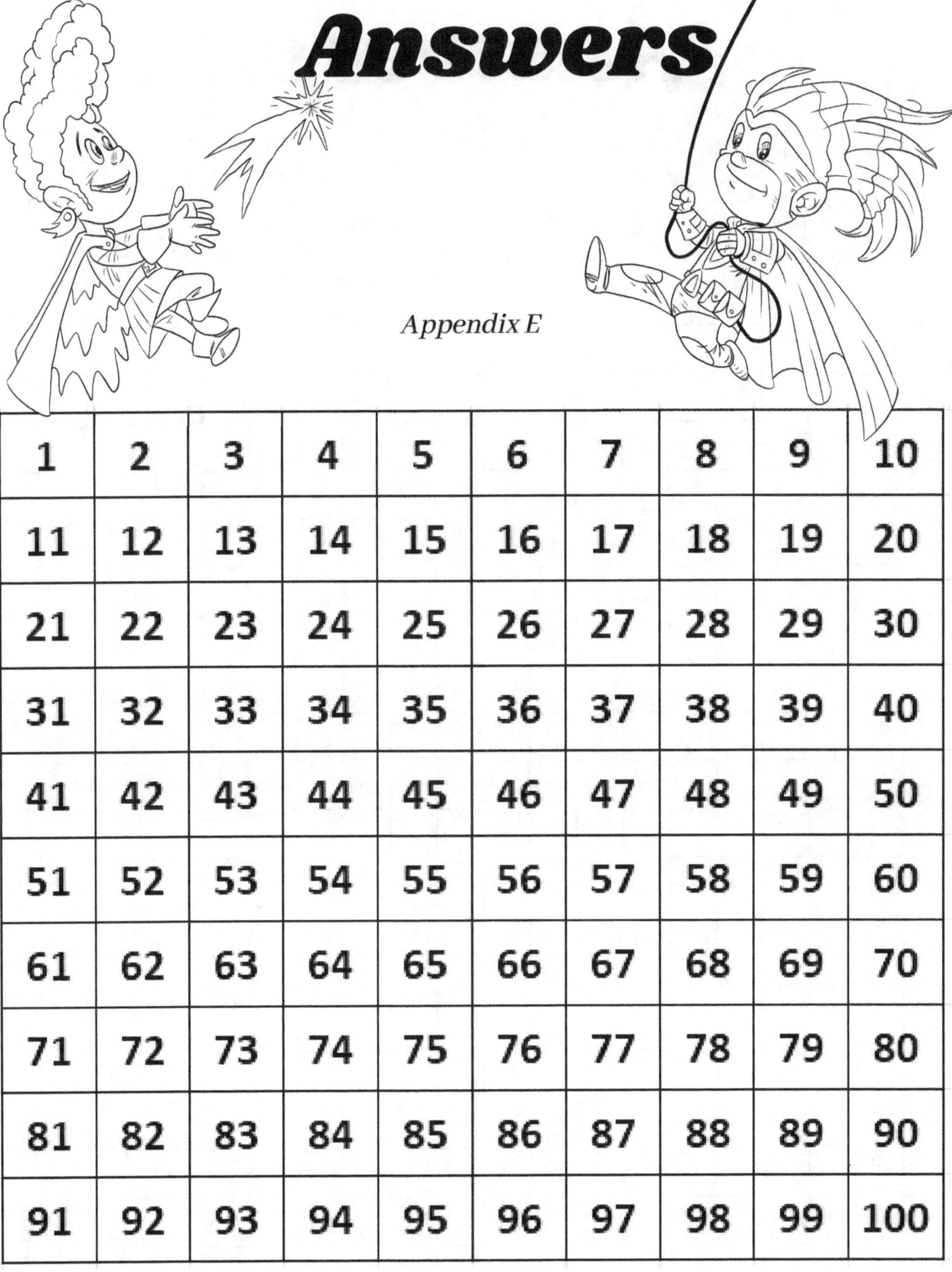

1	2	3	4	5	6	7	8	9	10
11	12	13	14	15	16	17	18	19	20
21	22	23	24	25	26	27	28	29	30
31	32	33	34	35	36	37	38	39	40
41	42	43	44	45	46	47	48	49	50
51	52	53	54	55	56	57	58	59	60
61	62	63	64	65	66	67	68	69	70
71	72	73	74	75	76	77	78	79	80
81	82	83	84	85	86	87	88	89	90
91	92	93	94	95	96	97	98	99	100

Answers

Appendix - F

Answers

Appendix - G

Answers

Appendix - H

Answers

Appendix - I